Wien · Vienna gestern und heute | then and now

László Lugo Lugosi

Wien
gestern und heute

Vienna
then and now

Herausgegeben von / *Edited by* Maria Emberger
Kommentar von / *Comments by* Alexander Pointner

SALZBURG 2006
EDITION FOTOHOF, OTTO MÜLLER VERLAG

Vorwort der Herausgeberin

Ein Spaziergang durch Wien ist auch eine Reise in die Vergangenheit. Wahrscheinlich haben wir alle schon einmal davon geträumt, einen Augenblick dieser Vergangenheit wirklich zu erleben.

Als Mitte des 19. Jahrhunderts das Verfahren der Fotografie der Öffentlichkeit vorgestellt wurde (1839, Daguerreotypie), war das Erstaunen der Betrachter vor allem auf die Detailgenauigkeit und Authentizität des Abgebildeten gerichtet. Die ersten Fotografen experimentierten mit Chemie und Optik und stellten ihre Kameras der Einfachheit halber ans Fenster. So sind die ersten erhalten gebliebenen Fotografien Stadtansichten, vom Fenster der Wissenschaftler aus gesehen. Die historischen Aufnahmen von Wien um 1900, die im vorliegenden Buch versammelt sind, zeigen vor allem die repräsentative Architektur der Ringstraßenära, die auch heute noch das Stadtbild prägt.

Obwohl wir mittlerweile an die Betrachtung von Fotografien gewohnt sind, überraschen uns manche Bilder durch ihre Magie. Die Magie, die diese Bilder begleitet, liegt im Verfahren der Fotografie selbst. Tatsächlich finden wir in den Bildern die Lichtstrahlen von wenigen Sekunden vor über hundert Jahren konserviert. Das Licht, das in einem Moment vor hundert Jahren durch das Objektiv auf eine Glasplatte getroffen ist, hat in der Emulsion eine chemische Reaktion ausgelöst, die noch heute sichtbar für uns ist.

Die Idee von László Lugo Lugosi dazu ist genau so einfach wie poetisch. Er wiederholt den Augenblick hundert Jahre später. Er spürt dem historischen Lichtstrahl nach, der heute in nur leicht veränderter Form auf seinen Film trifft. Und wieder wird ein Augenblick (diesmal ein Bruchteil einer Sekunde) für uns angehalten und konserviert. Zwei eingefrorene Momente machen erst im Vergleich die Zeit spürbar. Eine Rückschau um hundert Jahre schärft den Blick für das Heute. Fotografien von Wien um 1900 zeigen eine Stadt, die gleichzeitig fremd und sehr vertraut wirkt. In der Gegenüberstellung von historischen Stadtansichten mit identen Aufnahmen aus den Jahren 2005/06 findet der verloren geglaubte Moment eine Wiederkehr.

László Lugo Lugosi wählte Motive von alten Fotografien und Fotopostkarten, die einen außergewöhnlichen Vergleich mit der Gegenwart ermöglichen. Die Bilder stammen aus der Sammlung Seemann, Wien, aus der Postkartensammlung des „Zempléni Muzem", Szerencs, Ungarn, und aus seiner eigenen Sammlung. Fotografien, die still, statisch und repräsentativ wirken, sind charakteristisch für das 19. Jahrhundert. Der Fotograf hat solche Fotos den Bildern mit ungewöhnlichen Blickwinkeln oder originellen Schnappschüssen vorgezogen.

Ein imaginärer Spaziergang führt den Betrachter von der Innenstadt bis in die Außenbezirke, wobei die Bildpaare einen spannenden Vergleich zwischen dem Gestern und Heute ermöglichen. An einigen Bildpaaren sind massive Änderungen im Stadtbild festzustellen, an anderen wiederum fallen Unterschiede erst nach genauem Hinsehen auf. Der Kommentar von Alexander Pointner unterstützt die visuelle Erfahrung und beleuchtet die Szene mit kompakter Information. Der Blick des Betrachters wird geschärft und die historische Distanz überwunden.

Maria Emberger, Salzburg 2006

Preface by the Editor

A walk through Vienna is also a journey into the past. We have probably all once dreamt of experiencing an actual moment of this past. When the process of photography was introduced to the public (1839, Daguerreotype) in the mid-19th Century, the viewers were primarily fascinated by the exactness of detail and the authenticity of the representation. The first photographers experimented with chemistry and optics and, for the sake of ease, stood their cameras at their windows. And so, the first photographs that were preserved were views of cities taken from the windows of these scientists. The historical photographs of Vienna around 1900 that are assembled in this book, above all depict the representative architecture of the Ringstraßen-era, that still characterizes the cityscape today.

Even though we have all become accustomed to looking at photographs, some pictures still surprise us with their magic. The magic of these pictures stems from the process of photography itself. In these pictures, we actually discover preserved light rays that lasted several seconds over a hundred years ago. The light that traveled through the lens onto a glass plate one instant a hundred years ago, triggered a chemical reaction in the emulsion that remains visible for us today.

László Lugo Lugosi's idea in this regard is as simple as it is poetic. He repeats the same instant a hundred years later. He retraces the historical light ray that meets his film in an only slightly altered form today. And once again an instant (this time a fraction of a second) is captured and preserved for us. Time becomes palpable only when the two frozen moments are compared. Looking back one hundred years sharpens one's view of the present. Photographs of Vienna taken around 1900 show a city that seems both alien and familiar at the same time. By placing historical city views beside identical photographs taken in 2005 and 2006 seemingly lost moments suddenly return.

László Lugo Lugosi selected subjects from old photographs and postcards that make interesting comparisons with the present possible. The pictures stem from the Seemann Collection, Vienna, the postcard collection of the „Zempléni Muzem", Szerencs, Hungary, and from his own collection. Photographs that strike one as quiet, static, and representative are characteristic of the 19th century. Such photographs were favored over photographs with unusual perspectives or unique snapshots.

An imaginary walk takes the observer from the inner city to the outlying districts, with the image pairs enabling an exciting comparison between then and now. In some image pairs, dramatic changes in the cityscape can be detected, in others, however, differences only become noticeable upon closer inspection. Alexander Pointner's commentary supports the visual experience and illuminates the scene with compact information. The observer's view is sharpened and the historical distance is overcome.

Maria Emberger, Salzburg 2006

Bildpaare | Picture Pairs

01 Stephansdom
St. Stephen's Cathedral

02

Capistrankanzel am Stephansdom
Capistran Pulpit, St. Stephen's Cathedral

03   Stock-im-Eisen

04   **Donnerbrunnen**
Donner Fountain

05   Kapuzinerkirche
Capuchin Church

06   Kärntnerstraße

07   Albertina

08 Neues Burgtor
    New Castle Gate

09   **In der Burg**
      In der Burg Square

10   Schweizertor
       Swiss Gate

11   Josephsplatz

12   **Heldenplatz**
Heroes' Square

13   Maria-Theresien-Platz

14 Naturhistorisches Museum
    Natural History Museum

15   **Parlament**
Parliament

16   Kaiserin Elisabeth Denkmal
Memorial to Empress Elisabeth

17   Burgtheater

18 Rathaus
City Hall

19   Votivkirche

20   **Börse**
Stock Exchange

21   Maria am Gestade
Mary on the Strand

22   Am Hof

23   Graben

24   Hoher Markt

25 Heiligenkreuzerhof

26 Donaukanal
Danube Canal

27 Schwedenbrücke

28   Urania

29   **Wirtschaftsministerium**
Ministry of Economics

30 Wiental im Stadtpark
Wiental in the City Park

31   Stadtpark
Vienna City Park

32   Kursalon

33   Hochstrahlbrunnen am Schwarzenbergplatz
Rising Jet Fountain, Schwarzenbergplatz

34   Lothringerstraße

35 Musikverein

36   Karlskirche
      Church of St. Charles Borromeo

37 **Oper**
Opera

38   Opernring
         Opera Ring

39 Akademie der bildenden Künste am Schillerplatz
Academy of Fine Arts, Schillerplatz

40   Secession

41   Naschmarkt

42 Linke Wienzeile
Left Wienzeile

43   Wiedner Hauptstraße

44   **Mozartbrunnen**
Mozart Fountain

45   Margarethenplatz

46   **Flohmarkt**
Flea Market

47 Mariahilferstraße

48   **Volkstheater**
People's Theater

49   Jörgerbad

50 Hernals

51   Währingerstraße

52   Volksoper
          People's Opera

53   Strudelhofstiege
Strudelhof Steps

54   Roßauer Lände

55   Praterstern

56   Riesenrad
      Ferris Wheel

57   Volksprater

58   Lusthaus
         Pleasure House

59   Schönbrunn

60   Kahlenberg

Kommentar | Comments

01 Stephansdom
St. Stephen's Cathedral

Der Blick vom Graben auf den Stephansdom zeigt uns das wohl berühmteste österreichische Wahrzeichen: den „Steffl" genannten Südturm des Domes. Der zwischen 1359 und 1433 erbaute, 137 m hohe und sich nach oben hin verjüngende Turm ist eine ins Monumentale gesteigerte gotische Architektursculptur. Mit seiner reichen Bauplastik aus Sandstein stellt er eine permanente restauratorische Herausforderung dar. Als Wahrzeichen jüngeren Datums kann man das nach Plänen von Hans Hollein 1985–90 erbaute „Haas Haus" an der Ecke Graben/Stephansplatz bezeichnen.

The view from the Graben to St. Stephen's reveals to us what is probably Austria's most famous landmark: the "Steffl" (Little Stephen) as the Viennese call the South Tower of the cathedral. The 137 meter/450 ft high tower which was built between 1359 and 1433 and tapers with height, is a Gothic architectural sculpture of monumental proportions. With its richly ornamented sandstone sculptures, it represents a permanent challenge to conservators. The "Haas Haus" which was built between 1985 and 1990 at the corner of Graben and Stephansplatz according to plans by Hans Hollein can be described as a younger landmark.

02 Capistrankanzel am Stephansdom
Capistran Pulpit, St. Stephen's Cathedral

Die so genannte Capistrankanzel am Nord-Chor des Stephansdoms ist nach dem hl. Johannes von Capistran benannt, der dort im 15. Jh. seine kämpferischen Predigten gegen die Türken hielt. Das 1738 von Johann Josef Resler errichtete Denkmal zeigt den als „Apostel Europas" bekannten Franziskaner in heroischer Siegespose auf einem besiegten Türken stehend. Auffällig ist die heute leere Nische links neben dem Denkmal: hier befand sich das als Hutstockersche Kreuztragung bezeichnete Epitaph von 1523, das im 2. Weltkrieg zerstört wurde.

The so-called Capistrankanzel (Capistran pulpit) at the north choir of St. Stephen's Cathedral is named after St. John Capistran, who held his pugnacious sermons against the Turks there in the 15th century. The monument erected in 1738 by Johann Josef Resler depicts the Franciscan, known as the "Apostle of Europe," in a correspondingly heroic pose as a victor standing over a conquered Turk. Noteworthy is the niche to the left of the monument that is empty today: this is where the epitaph of 1523, known as the Hutstocker Kreuztragung (Carrying of the Cross) was located until it was destroyed during the Second World War.

03   Stock-im-Eisen

Beim Stock-im-Eisen, dessen erste urkundliche Erwähnung auf das Jahr 1533 zurückgeht, handelt es sich um einen 2,19 m hohen, auf einem Granitsockel stehenden Stamm, der an der Fassade des Palais Equitable, einem späthistoristischen Bürohaus am Eck zwischen Graben und Kärntnerstraße, angebracht ist. Dieser Nagelbaum geht auf einen Brauch durchreisender Schmiede und Schmiedgesellen zurück, sich mit einem Nagel zu verewigen. Der Wiener Stock-im-Eisen ist der älteste erhaltene Nagelbaum.

The "Stock-im-Eisen" is a 2,19 meter-high tree trunk mounted on a granite pedestal, that is attached to the façade of the Palais Equitable, an office building from the late Historicist period at the corner of the Graben and Kärntnerstraße. The tree trunk is first mentioned in a public document dating back to the year 1533. This "tree of nails" goes back to a usage by which traveling locksmiths and their apprentices immortalized themselves by hammering a nail into the tree trunk. The Vienna "Stock-im-Eisen" is the oldest preserved "tree of nails."

04   Donnerbrunnen
Donner Fountain

Der 1737–39 errichtete Providentia- oder Donner-Brunnen (benannt nach seinem Schöpfer Georg Raphael Donner) am Neuen Markt ist das älteste erhaltene, von der Gemeinde Wien beauftragte „Kunst-im-öffentlichen-Raum"-Projekt. Die Nacktheit der als vier Zubringerflüsse der Donau (Traun, Enns, March und Ybbs) bezeichneten Figuren am Bassinrand erregte solchen Anstoß, dass sie 1770 auf Befehl Maria Theresias für mehrere Jahrzehnte ins Depot wanderten. Heute sind die Bleifiguren längst durch Bronzekopien ersetzt. Die Originale sind im Unteren Belvedere ausgestellt.

The Providentia Fountain, or "Donner Fountain" (named after its builder Georg Raphael Donner) at the New Market is the oldest preserved "public art project" commissioned by the city of Vienna. The nudity of the four figures on the edge of the fountain's basin that symbolize the four tributaries of the Danube (Traun, Enns, March, and Ybbs) were so scandalous at the time that they were moved into the depot in 1770 on orders of Maria Theresia and stayed there for several decades. The original lead figures have long since been replaced by bronze replicas. The originals are now on show in the Lower Belvedere.

05 Kapuzinerkirche
Capuchin Church

Hinter der schlichten Fassade der 1617 von Kaiserin Anna gestifteten Kapuzinerkirche verbirgt sich die bedeutendste Gruft Österreichs, die Kaisergruft. Der 1657 verstorbene Ferdinand III. bestimmte sie offiziell zur letzten Ruhestätte der kaiserlichen Familie Habsburg. Unter den 146 Personen, die hier ihre letzte Ruhestätte gefunden haben, befinden sich 12 Kaiser und 19 Kaiserinnen. Die Fassade wurde letztmals 1933–36 verändert und mit Fresken von Rudolf Holzinger und Hans Fischer versehen.

Austria's most important tomb, the Kaisergruft (Imperial Crypt), is hidden behind the simple façade of the Kapuzinerkirche (Capuchin Church), founded in 1617 by Empress Anna. Ferdinand III who died in 1657 officially designated it as the final resting place of the Imperial family Habsburg. Among the 146 who have their final resting places here are 12 emperors and 19 empresses. The façade was altered in 1933–36 and decorated with frescoes by Rudolf Holzinger and Hans Fischer.

06 Kärntnerstraße

Der seit 1996 nach Herbert von Karajan benannte Platz vor der Oper markiert das Ende der Kärntnerstraße, vornehme Geschäftsstraße und längster Straßenzug der Innenstadt, die 1976 im Zuge des U-Bahn-Baues zur Fußgängerzone umfunktioniert wurde. Am mit Rund-Erkern versehenen Eckhaus, in dem sich einst das Café Scheidl befand, ist der so genannte Fenstergucker des 1859 geschliffenen Kärntnertores angebracht. Das 1861–63 errichtete Haus rechts für die ehemalige Bankiersfamilie Todesco markiert das früheste Beispiel für ein historistisches Palais mit reichem Skulpturenschmuck.

The square in front of the State Opera named since 1996 after Herbert von Karajan marks the end of the Kärtnerstraße, the sophisticated shopping street and longest street of houses in the city center, pedestrianized in 1976 in the course of subway construction. The so-called Fenstergucker ("window peeker") of the Kärntnertor, razed in 1859, is mounted onto the corner building with the rounded bays, which at one time housed the Café Scheidl. The house to the right with opulent sculptural decoration, built 1861–63 for the Todesco financier's family, is the earliest example of a Historicist palace.

07 Albertina

Der 1864–69 nach dem Vorbild römischer Wandbrunnen errichtete Danubius- oder Albrechts-brunnen an der Stirnseite der Albrechtsrampe vor der Albertina geht aus einem Entwurf Moritz von Löhrs hervor. Der durch einen Bombentreffer heute verkürzte Brunnen wird vom bronze-nen Reiterstandbild des Feldmarschalls Erzherzog Albrecht (von Caspar von Zumbusch, 1899) überragt und seit 2003 von einem von Hans Hollein entworfenen Flugdach namens „Soravia Wing", der das Dach des neu gestalteten Eingangsbereichs zur Albertina ziert.

The Danubius or Albrecht Fountain on the front side of the Albrechtsrampe in front of the Albertina was modeled on a Roman wall fountain and constructed in 1864–69 according to a design by Moritz von Löhr. The bronze equestrian statue of Archduke Albrecht (by Caspar von Zumbusch, 1899) towers over the fountain, which was reduced in size by a bomb strike; since 2003, a flying roof – designed by Hans Hollein and called "Soravia Wing" that adorns the roof of the newly constructed entrance area to the Albertina – towers over the fountain.

08 Neues Burgtor
New Castle Gate

Die Baugeschichte von Michaelertrakt und Neuem Burgtor zog sich länger als 150 Jahre hin. Der Plan von Joseph Emanuel Fischer von Erlach für den stadtseitigen Eingang zur Hofburg am Michaelerplatz stammt bereits aus dem Jahr 1725. Realisiert wurde er aber erst 1889–93 durch Ferdinand Kirschner, der auch einen alten Plan Nicolaus Pacassis, der drei Kuppeln vorsah, in die Ausführung miteinbezog. Beliebtes Fotomotiv ist der monumentale, der kon-kaven Fassade vorgelagerte späthistoristische Skulpturenschmuck: links und rechts zwei Brunnen („Macht zur See" und „Macht zu Lande") und um das Burgtor vier Herkulesgruppen.

The construction history of the Michaeler Tract and the Neues Burgtor lasted for over 150 years. Joseph Emanuel Fischer von Erlach's plans for the city-side entrance to the Imperial Palace on the Michaelerplatz dates already from 1725. It was only realized, however, from 1889–93 by Ferdinand Kirschner, who also incorporated an old plan of Nicolaus Pacassi which envisioned 3 cupolas. A favorite photo motif is the monumenal Late Historicist sculptural decoration in front of the concave façade: left and right two fountains ("Might at Sea" and "Might on Land") and four Hercules groups around the Burgtor.

09 In der Burg
In der Burg Square

Das nach Plänen von Pompeo Marchesi 1846 vollendete Denkmal für Kaiser Franz I. gilt als bedeutendstes Monument des Wiener Spätklassizismus. Der mit zahlreichen Allegorien und in antiker Gewandung dargestellte Kaiser steht im Zentrum des Platzes „In der Burg", dem einzigen großen Rechteckplatz des Hofburgensembles, der komplett von Trakten der Hofburg umschlossen ist. Hinter dem Kaiserdenkmal ist links die um 1600 entstandene Amalienburg und rechts der hochbarocke, 1723–30 von Joseph Emanuel Fischer von Erlach errichtete Reichskanzleitrakt zu sehen.

The Emperor Franz I memorial, built according to plans by Pompeo Marchesi in 1846, is considered the most important monument of late Viennese Neo-classicism. The emperor, depicted in antique garb and with numerous allegorical figures, stands in the center of the In der Burg square, the only large rectangular square of the Hofburg ensemble that is completely surrounded by Hofburg tracts. To the left behind the monument of the emperor is the Amalienburg, which was constructed around 1600; to the right is the High Baroque wing of the Imperial Chancellery built from 1723–30 by Joseph Emanuel Fischer von Erlach.

10 Schweizertor
Swiss Gate

Durch das im Inneren Burghof der Wiener Hofburg gelegene Schweizertor gelangt man in den Schweizerhof, wo sich die gotische Burgkapelle und die Schatzkammer befinden. Das monumentale Portal mit seiner markanten Schwarz-Rot-Gold-Färbung und dem bekrönenden Reichsadlerwappen König Ferdinands I. war Teil einer mittelalterlichen Toranlage, die 1552/53 errichtet wurde. Der gekrönte Steinlöwe im Vordergrund trägt das Wappen Österreichs.

The Schweizerhof (Swiss Courtyard) is reached through the Schweizer Tor (Swiss Gate) located in the inner courtyard of the Vienna Hofburg (Imperial Palace), where the Gothic palace chapel – Burgkapelle – and the treasury are located. The monumental portal with its distinctive black-red-gold coloring and the crowning Reichs-eagle coat of arms of King Ferdinand I was part of a medieval gate complex that was erected in 1552/53. The crowned stone lion in the foreground is wearing the Austrian coat of arms.

11 Josephsplatz

Kaiser Joseph II. wird zwar ganz nach dem Vorbild des Reiterstandbildes von Kaiser Marc Aurel am Kapitol in Rom in antiker Feldherrntracht dargestellt. In den Bronzereliefs am Sockel jedoch repräsentiert er den Reformkaiser, der Handel und Landwirtschaft fördert. Hinterfangen wird das 1807 enthüllte klassizistische Reiterstandbild von Franz Anton Zauner links vom Prunksaaltrakt (1722–26 von Johann Bernhard und Joseph Emanuel Fischer von Erlach) und rechts vom Redoutensaaltrakt (um 1769 von Nicolaus Pacassi) der Wiener Hofburg. Der zur Nationalbibliothek gehörende Prunksaal ist ein einzigartiger Barockraum für mehr als 200.000 Bücher.

Emperor Joseph II is represented in the tradition of the equestrian statue of Emperor Marcus Aurelius on the Capitoline in Rome, dressed as a Roman general. On the bronze reliefs on the pedestal, however, he is represented as the reformer emperor who promotes trade and agriculture. Franz Anton Zauner's Neoclassical equestrian statue, unveiled in 1807, is backed to the left by the Prunksaal tract (1722–26 by Johann Bernhard and Joseph Emanuel Fischer von Erlach) and to the right by the Redoutensaal tract (around 1769 by Nicolaus Pacassi) of the Hofburg (Imperial Palace). The Prunksaal (ceremonial hall) is part of the National Library and is a unique Baroque space for more than 200,000 books.

12 Heldenplatz
Heroes' Square

Der Heldenplatz erhielt 1865 nach der Aufstellung der beiden Reiterstandbilder von Anton Dominik Fernkorn seinen Namen. Die zuvor als Äußerer Burgplatz oder Paradeplatz bezeichnete großflächige Platzanlage liegt zwischen dem Volksgarten und der nach Plänen von Gottfried Semper und Carl von Hasenauer erst 1923 fertig gestellten Neuen Burg. Von den beiden Reiterstandbildern, die Prinz Eugen und Erzherzog Karl darstellen, gilt letzteres wegen seines auf den Hinterbeinen aufgerichteten Pferdes als statische Meisterleistung.

The Heldenplatz (Heroes' Square) received its name 1865 following the erection of the two equestrian statues by Anton Dominik Fernkorn. The extensive square, known earlier as the Outer Burgplatz or Parade Grounds, lies between the Volksgarten and the Neue Burg, completed only in 1923 following plans by Gottfried Semper and Carl von Hasenauer. Of the two equestrian statues representing Prince Eugen and Archduke Karl, the second, because of the horse standing on its hind legs, is considered to be a masterstroke of statics.

13 Maria-Theresien-Platz

Im Zentrum des Maria-Theresien-Platzes thront die Kaiserin an der Spitze eines nach Plänen Caspar von Zumbuschs 1888 enthüllten Gruppendenkmals. Das komplexe Figurenprogramm zeigt Repräsentanten aus Politik, Militär, Justiz, Wissenschaft und Kunst, die alle aus der Zeit Maria Theresias stammen. So ist etwa auch Wolfgang Amadeus Mozart als Knabe dargestellt. Im Hintergrund sind die ehemaligen, heute zum Museumsquartier umgebauten Hofstallungen zu sehen und rechts das Naturhistorische Museum.

At the center of Maria-Theresien-Platz the Empress is enthroned at the summit of a group monument designed by Caspar von Zumbusch, unveiled in 1888. The complex figural program includes representatives from politics, the military, the judiciary, science and the arts, all from the time of Maria Theresia. Wolfgang Amadeus Mozart is also portrayed as a child. In the background are the former Imperial Stables, recently converted into the Museum Quarter, and to the right is the Natural History Museum.

14 Naturhistorisches Museum
Natural History Museum

Das Naturhistorische Museum ist wie das gegenüberliegende Kunsthistorische Museum nach Plänen Carl von Hasenauers und Gottfried Sempers im Stil der Neorenaissance errichtet worden. Die beiden symmetrisch angeordneten Museumsbauten flankieren den nach barocken Vorbildern von Hofgärtner Adolf Vetter gestalteten Maria-Theresien-Platz, dessen Zentrum das monumentale Denkmal der Kaiserin bildet. Dieses herausragende Beispiel eines gründerzeitlichen Gartenplatzes wurde 1888 am Geburtstag Maria Theresias eröffnet.

The Natural History Museum, like the Museum of Fine Arts opposite, was built in the Neo-Renaissance style according to plans by Carl von Hasenauer and Gottfried Semper. The two symmetrically arranged museum buildings flank the Maria-Theresien-Platz, designed in a Baroque manner by the Imperial Gardener Adolf Vetter, at the center of which stands the monumental memorial to the Empress. This outstanding example of a "foundation era" garden square was inaugurated in 1888 on Maria Theresia's birthday.

15 Parlament
Parliament

Das vom Typus mit dem Kapitol in Washington vergleichbare Parlament gilt als wichtigstes Werk des Architekten Theophil von Hansen und als herausragender Monumentalbau des Wiener Ringstraßen-Ensembles. Zwischen 1871 und 1883 wurde es in Anlehnung an antike Tempel errichtet und mit einem umfangreichen Skulpturenprogramm ausgestattet. Die mächtigste davon ist die Pallas Athene vom gleichnamigen Brunnen von Karl Kundmann, um den eine doppelarmige, erst 2005 sanierte Auffahrtsrampe zum Säulenportikus führt.

The Parliament, comparable in type to the Capitol in Washington, is considered the most important work of the architect Theophil von Hansen. It is also an outstanding monumental part of the Viennese Ringstraße ensemble. It was built in allusion to antique temples and equipped with a comprehensive sculptural program. The most massive of which is the Pallas Athena and the so named fountain built by Karl Kundmann, around which a double-armed ramp, restored only in 2005, leads to the column portico.

16 Kaiserin Elisabeth-Denkmal
Memorial to Empress Elisabeth

Das Denkmal der Kaiserin Elisabeth bildet den nördlichen Abschluss des Volksgartens. Im Hintergrund ist das Burgtheater zu erkennen. Dem Elisabeth-Denkmal ging eine sechsjährige Vorgeschichte voraus, in der trotz zweimaligem Wettbewerb kein Sieger nominiert werden konnte. Schließlich erhielt der Architekt Friedrich Ohrmann 1903 außer Konkurrenz den Zuschlag. Mit der Ausführung der 2,5 m hohen, thronenden, nur als Privatmensch charakterisierten Kaiserin wurde Hans Bitterlich betraut. 1907, neun Jahre nach Elisabeths Tod, wurde das Denkmal eröffnet.

The memorial to Empress Elisabeth encloses the northern end of the Volksgarten (People's Garden). The Burgtheater can be seen in the background. During the six years predating the building of the memorial to Elisabeth, two competitions were held during which no winner could be nominated. Finally, the architect Friedrich Ohrmann was awarded the commission in 1903 outside of the competition. Hans Bitterlich was consigned with the construction of the 2,5 m high, throned empress, depicted as a private citizen. The monument was unveiled in 1907, nine years after Elisabeth's death.

17 Burgtheater

Das seit 1919 schlicht Burgtheater genannte ehemalige K.K. Hofburgtheater ist unter Kaiser Joseph II. 1776 als „Teutsches Nationaltheater" gegründet worden. Der heutige Bau in Neorenaissanceformen wurde im Zuge des Ringstraßenausbaus gegenüber dem Rathaus zwischen 1874 und 1888 errichtet. Gottfried Semper war für den Entwurf verantwortlich, Carl von Hasenauer für die Ausführung. Bereits im 19. Jh. erwarb sich das bedeutendste Theater Wiens den Ruf, eine der großen Sprechbühnen Europas zu sein.

The Imperial Royal Court Theater, known simply as the „Burgtheater" since 1919, was founded 1776 under Emperor Joseph II as the "Teutsches Nationaltheater" (German National Theater). Today's Neo-Renaissance theater was constructed between 1874 and 1888 in the course of the expansion of the Ringstraße across from City Hall. Gottfried Semper was responsible for the design and Carl von Hasenauer for the construction. Already in the 19th Century, Vienna's most important theater had acquired the reputation of being one of the great stages in Europe.

18 Rathaus
City Hall

Der Sitz des Bürgermeisters, das Wiener Rathaus, ist ein herausragender Monumentalbau der Neogotik und wurde 1872–83 vom Architekten und Dombaumeister Friedrich von Schmidt errichtet. Mit dem zum Wiener Wahrzeichen gewordenen „Eisernen Rathausmann" misst sein Turm über 100 m. Am vom Rathauspark gesäumten und zur Ringstraße hin offenen Platz finden das ganze Jahr über Veranstaltungen statt. Die traditionellste und beliebteste davon ist der Christkindlmarkt zur Weihnachtszeit.

City Hall, the seat of the mayor, is a prominent Neo-Gothic building, constructed between 1872–83 by the architect and cathedral builder Friedrich von Schmidt. With its iron figure – the "Rathausmann" – a Vienna landmark – the tower stands more than 100 meters tall. Events take place all year round on the square, which is lined by the town hall park and opens out toward the Ringstraße. The most traditional and beloved event is the annual Advent Market at Christmastime.

19 Votivkirche

Hinter dem weiten, heute als Sigmund-Freud-Park bezeichneten Dreiecksplatz zwischen Universitäts- und Währingerstraße ragt die imposante Doppelturmfassade der Votivkirche in den Himmel. Die sich in einer Achse zum Schottentor befindliche Kirche ist eigentlich ein Denkmal, das Kaiser Franz Joseph zum Gedächtnis an seine Errettung von einem Attentat 1853 errichten ließ. Der 1879 vollendete neogotische Bau von Heinrich von Ferstel gilt als Höhepunkt historistischer Sakralarchitektur in Wien.

Behind the wide triangular space between the Universitätsstraße and Währingerstraße, known today as Sigmund-Freud-Park, the imposing twin spires of the Votivkirche rise into the sky. The church, on an axis to the Schottentor, is actually a monument, erected by Emperor Franz Joseph in memory of an aborted assassination attempt on his life in 1853. The Neo-Gothic building by Heinrich von Ferstel, completed in 1879, is one of the highlights of Historicist ecclesiastical architecture in Vienna.

20 Börse
Stock Exchange

Erst gut 100 Jahre nach ihrer Gründung am 1. August 1771 erhielt die Börse am Schottenring einen repräsentativen Sitz. Der 1877 nach Plänen von Theophil von Hansen in Renaissanceformen vollendete Bau zeigt die für diesen Architekten typischen vorspringenden Ecktürme die u.a. auch an der Akademie der bildenden Künste angebracht sind.
Der 1956 durch einen Brand zerstörte Börsesaal wurde von Erich Boltenstern neu gestaltet. Vom gleichen Architekten stammt auch der im Hintergrund zu sehende Ringturm. Er ist das erste Bürohochhaus Wiens.

It was not until a century after its founding on August 1st, 1771 that the Stock Exchange on the Schottenring obtained a representative place of business. Constructed according to plans by Theophil von Hansen and completed in 1877, the Renaissance-style building possesses protruding corner towers, so typical for this architect and similar to those attached to the Academy of Fine Arts. The stock exchange hall was destroyed by fire in 1956 and reconstructed by Erich Boltenstern. The "Ring Tower," built by the same architect, was Vienna's first office high-rise and can be seen in the background.

21

Maria am Gestade
Mary on the Strand

Die inmitten engster Verbauung ganz unvermutet auftauchende Kirche Maria am Gestade ist einer der bedeutendsten gotischen Sakralbauten Wiens. Ihre ehemalige Lage am Steilabfall zur Donau machte die Errichtung einer Stiege zum Tiefen Graben notwendig, die in ihrer heutigen Form aus dem Jahr 1937 stammt und wegen ihrer Länge gerne für Hochzeiten verwendet wird. Am markantesten an der Ordenskirche der Redemptoristen (seit 1820) ist ihr 1429 vollendeter Turm, der auch auf den ältesten Stadtveduten abgebildet ist.

In the middle of a highly developed area, the Kirche Maria am Gestade (Mary on the Strand Church) appears unexpectedly, yet is one of Vienna's most important gothic ecclesiastical buildings. Its former location on the steep banks of the Danube necessitated the building of a stairway to the Tiefer Graben, built in today's form in 1937 and, because of its length, popular for weddings. The most distinctive feature of the minster of the Redemptorists (since 1820) is its tower, completed in 1429 and included in the oldest views of the city.

22

Am Hof

Der Am Hof genannte Platz ist einer der historisch bemerkenswertesten der Wiener Innenstadt. Bereits in der Antike war er Teil des Römerlagers und um die Mitte des 12. Jh. wurde hier unter Heinrich II. Jasomirgott die Babenbergerresidenz gegründet. 1806 wurde von der Terrasse der Kirche am Hof die Auflösung des Hl. Römischen Reichs deutscher Nation proklamiert. Um die 1646 im Zentrum des Platzes aufgestellte Mariensäule gruppieren sich mehrere kunsthistorisch bedeutende Gebäude von der Renaissance bis zum Historismus, deren Substanz trotz erheblicher Bombenschäden weitgehend erhalten werden konnte.

The square known as „Am Hof" is one of the historically most remarkable sites in the Vienna city center. Already in antiquity, Romans set up camp here and in the middle of the 12th century, the Babenberger Residence was founded here under Heinrich II Jasomirgott. In 1806, the dissolution of the Holy Roman Empire of the German Nation was proclaimed from the terrace of the church at Am Hof. Several architecturally noteworthy buildings dating from the Renaissance to Historicism are grouped around the pillar with the figure of the Virgin Mary erected in the middle of the square in 1646. In spite of heavy bombing damage, these buildings have for the most part been well preserved.

23 Graben

Die in der Mitte des Grabens aufgestellte Pestsäule ist bis heute das größte öffentliche Monument Wiens. Sie geht auf ein Gelöbnis Kaiser Leopolds I. anlässlich der Pest von 1679 zurück. Zunächst von Johann Frühwirt nur in Holz ausgeführt, wurde sie danach von Matthias Rauchmiller und nach dessen Tod von Johann Bernhard Fischer von Erlach in Stein bis 1694 neu errichtet. Die 18 m hohe Säule mit ihren neun lebensgroßen Engeln und der bekrönenden Dreifaltigkeitsgruppe gilt als Initialwerk des Wiener Hochbarock.

The Plague Pillar erected at the center of the Graben is today still Vienna's largest public monument. It dates back to a vow made by Emperor Leopold I during the plague epidemic of 1679. Executed initially by Johann Frühwirt in wood, it was erected anew in stone by Matthias Rauchmiller and, following Rauchmiller's death, by Johann Bernhard Fischer von Erlach until 1694. The 18 m (59 ft) high column with its 9 life-size angels and the crowning Trinity group is considered to be a primary example of Viennese High Baroque.

24 Hoher Markt

Einer der ältesten Plätze Wiens war im Mittelalter Zentrum des bürgerlichen Wien und lange Zeit wichtigste Hinrichtungsstätte. Im Zentrum des über den Ruinen des ehemaligen Römerlagers Vindobona gelegenen Platzes steht der Vermählungs- oder Josefsbrunnen. Er ist der Hochzeit von Maria und Josef gewidmet und wurde 1729–32 von Joseph Emanuel Fischer von Erlach errichtet. Hauptattraktion des durch den Weltkrieg arg in Mitleidenschaft gezogenen Platzes ist aber die Ankeruhr (1911–17 von Franz Matsch), die jede volle Stunde eine andere Persönlichkeit aus der Wiener Geschichte zeigt.

The Hoher Markt, one of the oldest squares in the city, was the center of bourgeois Vienna during the Middle Ages, and for a long time the most important place of execution. At the center of the square, located above the ruins of the former Roman fortified encampment Vindobona, is the Espousal Fountain (or Josefsbrunnen). It is dedicated to the marriage of Mary and Joseph and was built 1729–32 by Joseph Emanuel Fischer von Erlach. However, the main attraction of the square, badly damaged during the World War, is the Ankeruhr (Anker Clock, 1911–17 by Franz Matsch), which presents a different figure from Viennese history on the hour.

25 Heiligenkreuzerhof

Die Bernhardskapelle ist Teil des Heiligenkreuzerhofes, eines heterogenen, bis ins Hochmittelalter zurückreichenden Baukomplexes, dessen Häuser noch heute zum Zisterzienserorden Heiligenkreuz gehören. Berühmt an der schlichten, 1662 errichteten Kapelle ist ihr hochbarocker, um 1730 entstandener Innenraum, für den u.a. die Maler Martino Altomonte und Paul Troger sowie der Bildhauer Giovanni Giuliani verantwortlich zeichneten. Überragt wird die Kapelle von den zwei Türmen der Jesuitenkirche.

The Bernhard Chapel is part of the Heiligenkreuzerhof, a heterogeneous building complex dating back to the High Middle Ages. Its buildings still belong to the Cistercian Order Heiligenkreuz (Holy Cross) today. The most famous part of the simple chapel, which was built in 1662, is the interior, which was created around 1730 during the High Baroque by the painters Martino Altomonte and Paul Troger as well as the sculptor Giovanni Giuliani. The two towers of the Jesuit church rise above the chapel.

26 Donaukanal
Danube Canal

Im Mittelalter floss der Hauptarm der Donau an der heutigen Wiener Innenstadt vorbei. Durch zahlreiche, das Flussbett verändernde Hochwasser verlegte sich der Hauptarm nach Osten, und so liegt der 1. Bezirk heute an einem Nebenarm, dem im Zuge der Donauregulierung um 1870 ausgebauten Donaukanal. Auf der Insel, die sich zwischen Donau und Donaukanal gebildet hat, liegen die Bezirke Leopoldstadt und Brigittenau. Sie sind mit der Altstadt durch Brücken, wie der hier nach 1945 erstmals in neuer Stahlbetontechnik errichteten Marienbrücke, verbunden.

In the Middle Ages, the main arm of the Danube flowed by what is Vienna's city center today. Through numerous floods, which altered the riverbed, the main arm shifted to the east, and so the 1st District now lies on a side arm, which was made into the Donaukanal during the course of the regulation of the Danube around 1870. The Leopoldstadt and Brigittenau Districts lie on the island that was formed between the Danube and the Donaukanal. They are connected to the Old Town by bridges, such as the Marienbrücke, erected after 1945 using modern reinforced concrete techniques for the first time.

27 Schwedenbrücke

Durch zahlreiche Bombentreffer wurden 1945 die Donaukanalbrücken und die Häuserzeilen beiderseits des Kanals fast zur Gänze zerstört. So auch die 1909–11 errichtete Ferdinands-brücke, die vom Franz-Josefs-Kai, der Verbindung zwischen Schotten- und Stubenring, in den 2. Bezirk führte. 1954/55 wurde sie erneuert und in Schwedenbrücke umbenannt, zum Dank für die Hilfe Schwedens in den Jahren nach dem 1. Weltkrieg, die besonders den Wiener Kindern zu Gute kam.

The Donaukanal bridges and the rows of houses on both sides of the canal were almost entirely destroyed by numerous bombing strikes in 1945. As was the Ferdinandsbrücke that was constructed from 1909–11 and leads from the Franz-Josefs-Kai – connecting the Schotten- and the Stubenring – to the 2nd District. In 1954/55 it was rebuilt and renamed "Schweden-brücke" in appreciation of Swedish aid during the years after the First World War, which bene-fitted above all Vienna's children.

28 Urania

Die nach der griechischen Muse der Astronomie benannte Urania steht an einem städtebau-lich markanten Platz, wo einander Ringstraße und Franz-Josefs-Kai kreuzen und der Wien-fluss in den Donaukanal mündet. Sie wurde 1909/10 von Max Fabiani als Volksbildungshaus und Theater (seit 1920 Kino), verbunden mit einer Sternwarte, erbaut und erst 2003 von Dimitris Manikas modernisiert, zu sehen v.a. an der Cafeteria aus einer Stahl-Glas-Konstruktion. Die niedrige Kassenhalle stammt aus den 30er Jahren. Die Wiener Kinder lieben die Urania beson-ders: sie ist Heimat des Kasperls.

Named after the Greek muse of astronomy, the Urania stands at an urbanistically important location, where the Ringstraße and Franz-Josefs-Kai intersect and the Wienfluß flows into the Donaukanal. It was built 1909/10 by Max Fabiani as a theater (since 1920 a cinema) and a public education center attached to an observatory. It was not modernized until 2003 by Dimitris Manikas; the steel-glass construction which houses the cafeteria is the most notable feature of this renovation. The low entrance hall was built in the thirties. Viennese children in particular love the Urania because it is the home of "Kasperl," the Austrian "Punch."

29 Wirtschaftsministerium
Ministry of Economics

Das ehemalige k.u.k. Reichskriegsministerium am Stubenring 1 gilt als letzter Monumentalbau der Wiener Ringstraße. Der aus dem heutigen Tschechien stammende Architekt Ludwig
Baumann zeichnete für den späthistoristischen, 1909–13 errichteten Bau verantwortlich. Vor
dem nunmehrigen Wirtschaftsministerium steht ein Denkmal des habsburgischen Kriegs-
helden Feldmarschall Graf Radetzky.

The former Imperial and Royal Ministry of War at Stubenring 1 is considered to be the last
monumental structure of the Vienna Ringstraße. The architect Ludwig Baumann from what is
today the Czech Republic, was responsible for the Late Historicist building, erected 1909–1913.
A monument to the Habsburg war hero Field Marshal Count Radetzky stands in front of the
building, today the Ministry of Economics.

30 Wiental
Wiental in the City Park

Der Wienfluss (schlicht „Wien" genannt) entspringt im westlichen Wienerwald und verläuft
im Stadtgebiet fast durchgehend in einem tiefen Betonbett, das 1895–99 errichtet wurde, um
die verheerenden Hochwässer zu verhindern. Bevor die Wien bei der Urania in den Donaukanal mündet, durchläuft sie den Stadtpark, dessen schöne Verbauung mit Flussportal, Pavillons und Ufertreppen 1903–07 von Friedrich Ormann und Josef Hackhofer gestaltet wurde.

The Wienfluss (Wien River, known simply as the Wien) has its source in the western Wienerwald (Vienna Woods). In the city limits it runs almost entirely in a deep concrete basin, built
1895-99 in order to prevent the devastating floods. Before the Wien flows into the Donaukanal
at the Urania it flows through the Stadtpark, whose lovely river portal, pavilions and embank-
ment steps were designed by Friedrich Ormann and Josef Hackhofer 1903–1907.

31 Stadtpark
Vienna City Park

Der vom Wienfluss durchquerte Stadtpark ist die erste und größte öffentliche Grünanlage der Innenstadt. Im ab 1860 als englischer Garten von Rudolph Siebeck konzipierten Park sind viele Künstler- und Musikerdenkmäler entlang der verschlungenen Wege aufgestellt.
Das Foto zeigt das 1898 von Josef Tilgner errichtete Denkmal für den Historien- und Bildnismaler Hans Makart, dessen Atelier 1870–80 das Zentrum des gesellschaftlichen Lebens in Wien war. Er ist hier mit dem Kostüm für den von Makart persönlich inszenierten Festzug anlässlich der Silberhochzeit des Kaiserpaares dargestellt.

The Stadtpark, through which the Wienfluss (Wien River) flows, is the earliest and largest public park in the city center. Numerous monuments to artists and musicians have been placed along the winding paths of the park which was designed by Rudolph Siebeck after 1860 in the English landscape garden style. The photo shows Josef Tilgner's 1898 memorial to the history painter and portraitist Hans Makart, whose studio was the center of Viennese social life from 1870–80. He is depicted here in a costume from the parade he orchestrated personally on the occasion of the Imperial couple's Silver Anniversary.

32 Kursalon

Der Kursalon ist ein im Stil eines barocken Gartenpalais erscheinendes Gebäude, das 1865 bis 1867 nach einem Entwurf Johannes Garbens errichtet wurde. Mit seinen Licht durchfluteten Seitentrakten und den Eckpavillons zitiert der im Wiener Stadtpark gelegene Prachtbau zwei prominente Vertreter Wiener Barockarchitektur: die Gloriette und das Obere Belvedere. Bis heute ist der Kursalon, in dem schon die Gebrüder Strauß ihre größten Erfolge feierten, prunkvoller Veranstaltungsort zahlreicher Bälle und führende Adresse Wiener Eventkultur.

The Kursalon is a building in the style of a Baroque garden palace, built 1865 to 1867 according to a design by Johannes Garben. With its light-filled side tracts and the corner pavilions the magnificent building in the Stadtpark of Vienna cites two prominent examples of Viennese Baroque architecture: the Gloriette and the Upper Belvedere. The Kursalon, where already the Brothers Strauß celebrated their greatest successes, is today still a splendid venue for numerous balls and an important address for Viennese event culture.

33 Hochstrahlbrunnen am Schwarzenbergplatz
Rising Jet Fountain, Schwarzenbergplatz

Der Charakter des von Anton Gabrielli, dem Erbauer der ersten Wiener Hochquellwasserleitung, gestifteten und 1873 eröffneten Hochstrahlbrunnen am Schwarzenbergplatz wurde zweimal entscheidend verändert. Zunächst 1906 durch seine Umgestaltung in einen Leuchtbrunnen und dann 1945, als vom sowjetischen Architekten Jakowiew und dem Bildhauer Intazarin ein Befreiungsdenkmal aufgestellt wurde. Es umfängt den Brunnen in der Mittelachse mit einem hohen, von einem Rotarmisten bekrönten Sockel und seitlich mit einer Kolonnade.

The character of the Hochstrahlbrunnen (rising jet fountain) on the Schwarzenbergplatz, donated by Anton Gabrielli, builder of the first Viennese Hochquellwasserleitung (high springs water conduit), and inaugurated in 1873, was significantly changed twice. First in 1906 when it was illuminated, and then in 1945, when a monument to the liberation of Vienna was erected by the Soviet architect Jakowiew and the sculptor Intazarin. It surrounds the fountain at the central axis with a high pedestal crowned by a soldier of the Red Army and to the side with a colonnade.

34 Lothringerstraße

Die heute mehrspurige, vom Karlsplatz zum Stadtpark führende Lothringerstraße dient zur Verkehrsentlastung der Ringstraße. Die repräsentative Verbauung in Richtung Schwarzenbergplatz mit fünfgeschossigen Mietshäusern ist unmittelbar nach der Wienflusseinwölbung um 1900 entstanden. Auf dem damals noch freien östlichen Abschnitt des Karlsplatzes steht seit 1959 das Wien-Museum Oswald Haerdtls.

The Lothringerstraße, which is a multi-lane street today, leads from the Karlsplatz to the Stadtpark and serves to reduce traffic on the Ringstraße. The representative construction with five-story apartment buildings toward the Schwarzenbergplatz was developed around 1900 immediately after the vaulting over of the Wienfluss. Since 1959, Oswald Haerdtl's Vienna Museum has stood on the Karlsplatz's eastern side, which was still vacant at the time.

35 Musikverein

Der Musikverein wurde nach Plänen von Theophil von Hansen 1867–70 für den Verein der Gesellschaft der Musikfreunde des österreichischen Kaiserreichs erbaut. Er gilt als Initialwerk für zahlreiche Bauten des Ringstraßenensembles in Neorenaissanceformen. 1911 wurden die Nischen des Erdgeschosses durch Fenster ersetzt und die Figuren großer Komponisten ins Innere transferiert. Der erhöhte Mitteltrakt beherbergt den so genannten Goldenen Saal, der für seine Akustik weltberühmt ist.

The Musikverein was built according to plans by Theophil von Hansen from 1867–70 for the Association of the Society of Friends of Music of the Austrian Empire. It is considered to be the inspiration for numerous Neo-Renaissance buildings of the Ringstraße. In 1911, the niches on the ground floor were replaced by windows, and the figures of great composers were moved indoors. The elevated middle tract houses the so-called Golden Hall whose acoustics are world famous.

36 Karlskirche
Church of St. Charles Borromeo

Ihre Entstehung verdankt die bedeutendste Barockkirche Wiens einem Gelöbnis Kaiser Karls VI., der die Karlskirche anlässlich der abgewendeten Pest von 1713 errichten ließ. Das Erscheinungsbild des nach Entwürfen Johann Bernhard Fischer von Erlachs 1739 fertig gestellten Baus wird von der mächtigen, im Inneren mit den berühmten Fresken Johann Michael Rottmayrs ausgestatteten Kuppel und den beiden nach römischem Vorbild gestalteten Triumphsäulen beherrscht. Links davon sieht man einen Teil des 1959 eröffneten „Wien Museum Karlsplatz" von Oswald Haerdtl. Es ist der erste Museumsneubau der 2. Republik.

Vienna's most important Baroque church owes its existence to a vow made by Emperor Karl VI, who had the Karlskirche built when the plague of 1713 was successfully warded off. The building's appearance, completed in 1739 after plans by Johann Bernhard Fischer von Erlach, is dominated by the mighty dome, decorated on the interior with the famous frescoes by Johann Michael Rottmayr, and by the two Triumphal Pillars based on Roman archetypes. To the left, part of the Wien Museum Karlsplatz by Oswald Haerdtl, opened in 1959, is visible. It is the first new museum building of the Second Republic.

37 Oper
Opera

Die hier von der Ecke Opernring/Kärntnerstraße aufgenommene Oper gilt als der erste staatliche Großbau an der Ringstraße und heute als eines der weltweit führenden Opernhäuser. Sie ist v.a. durch die imposante Loggia am Vorbau und ihre von führenden Wiener Künstlern ausgeführte Innenausstattung ein Höhepunkt des Romantischen Historismus und Hauptwerk des bedeutenden Architektenduos Siccardsburg/Van der Nüll, das allerdings dessen Vollendung 1869 nicht mehr miterleben konnte.

The opera, photographed here from the corner of Opernring/Kärnterstraße, is considered to be the first major state-built construction on the Ringstraße and to be one of the leading opera houses in the world. Its impressive loggia and its interior, painted by leading Viennese artists, is a highlight of Romantic Historicism and a major work of the famous architectural partners Siccardsburg/Van der Nüll, who unfortunately did not live to see its completion in 1869.

38 Opernring
Opera Ring

Der Opernring zwischen der Kärntnerstraße und der Eschenbachgasse ist das älteste, bereits 1861 eröffnete Teilstück der Ringstraße. Besonders im Bereich der Oper sind durch Bombentreffer viele Häuser zerstört worden. Das prominenteste Opfer war Theophil von Hansens Heinrichhof gegenüber der Oper. Er galt als bedeutendstes Zinspalais der Ringstraßenzeit. Sein 1954–56 errichteter Nachfolgerbau, der Opernringhof, stammt von den Architekten Carl Appel, Georg Lippert und Alfred Obiditisch.

The Opernring between Kärnterstraße and Eschenbachgasse is the oldest portion of the Ringstraße, opened already in 1861. Many houses were destroyed by bombs, particularly in the vicinity of the opera. The most prominent victim was the Heinrichhof by Theophil von Hansen across from the opera. Its successor building, the Opernringhof, was built between 1954–56 by the architects Carl Appel, Georg Lippert und Alfred Obiditisch.

39 Akademie der bildenden Künste am Schillerplatz
Academy of Fine Arts, Schillerplatz

Das nach einem Entwurf des Dresdner Bildhauers Johannes Schilling 1876 enthüllte Schiller-Denkmal steht im Zentrum der seit 1870 als Schillerplatz bezeichneten Parkanlage vor der Akademie der bildenden Künste. Die von Theophil von Hansen in Renaissanceformen erbaute Akademie wurde 1877 fertig gestellt. Auffallend ist die an den Palazzo Farnese in Rom angelehnte Fassadengestaltung mit ihren alternierenden Fenstern und Nischen mit Ädikularahmung, in die 24 Kopien antiker Götterstatuen eingestellt sind.

Unveiled in 1876 and constructed according to a design by the Dresden sculptor Johannes Schilling, the Schiller monument stands in the middle of the park in front of the Academy of Fine Arts, which has been known as the "Schillerplatz" (Schiller Square) since 1870. The Academy, built in the Renaissance style by Theophil von Hansen, was completed in 1877. Of note is the composition of the façade, reminiscent of the Palazzo Farnese in Rome with its alternating windows and niches with aedicular framing, into which 24 replicas of antique deities have been placed.

40 Secession

Die Secession mit ihrer markanten Goldkuppel aus eisernen Lorbeerblättern ist eines der bedeutendsten Werke des Jugendstils. Sie wurde 1897/98 von Josef Maria Olbrich als Vereinsgebäude für die aus der Künstlerhausgenossenschaft ausgetretene Vereinigung bildender Künstler Österreichs erbaut und ist auch heute noch Zentrum für Ausstellungen zeitgenössischer Kunst. Im Kellerraum beherbergt sie den berühmten Beethovenfries von Gustav Klimt. Als wesentliche bauliche Veränderung ist im Hintergrund der von Roland Rainer und Gustav Peichl 1993–95 als Dependance der Akademie der bildenden Künste errichtete Akademiehof zu erkennen.

The Secession with its distinctive golden cupola of iron bay leaves is one of the most important buildings of the Art Nouveau. It was constructed in 1897/98 by Josef Maria Olbrich as a building for the Association of Visual Artists who had resigned from the Artists' Cooperative Society, and it still remains a center for contemporary art exhibitions. The lower floor houses Gustav Klimt's famous Beethoven frieze. A major architectural addition can be noted in the background: the Akademiehof, which was constructed by Roland Rainer and Gustav Peichl from 1993–95 as a dependency of the Academy of Fine Arts.

41 Naschmarkt

Ab 1902 wurden die ersten Pavillons des zwischen Rechter und Linker Wienzeile, Getreidemarkt und Kettenbrückengasse gelegenen Naschmarktes nach Plänen von Friedrich Jäckel erbaut. Bevor Wiens bekanntester Obst- und Gemüsemarkt um 1900 auf die Wienflussüberdachung übersiedelte, lag er am Beginn der Wiedner Hauptstraße, wo es eine Aschenlagerstätte gab. Deswegen hieß der Markt auch früher Aschenmarkt, auf dem u.a. Holzasche zum Reinigen von Geschirr verkauft wurde.

From 1902 on the first pavilions of the Naschmarkt, located between the Right and Left Wienzeile, the Getreidemarkt and the Kettenbrückengasse, were built according to plans by Friedrich Jäckel. Before moving to the covering of the Wienfluss (Wien River), Vienna's best-known fruit and vegetable market was located at the beginning of the Wiedner Hauptstraße, where there was also a storage place for ashes. Therefore, the market was also called the ash market, where wood ash was sold for cleaning crockery.

42 Linke Wienzeile
Left Wienzeile

Die 1898/99 an der Linken Wienzeile errichteten Gebäude Nr. 38 und 40 (so genanntes Majolikahaus) gelten als das bedeutendste Mietshausensemble Otto Wagners. Die sechsgeschossigen Zinshäuser sind wegen ihres reichen secessionistischen Dekors – besonders das Majolikahaus mit seiner floralen Dekoration in Rosa-Grün-Blau – weltbekannt. Neben Wagner wirkten die wichtigsten seiner Schüler wie etwa Josef Plečnik und der Secessionskünstler Kolo Moser an der Ausführung des Gebäudekomplexes mit.

The buildings Nr. 38 and 40 constructed in 1898/99 on the Left Wienzeile are considered to be Otto Wagner's most important apartment house ensemble. The six-story buildings are world famous for their rich Secessionist décor – in particular the Majolikahaus with its floral decorations in pink, green, and blue. Wagner's most important students, such as Josef Plečnik and the Secessionist artist Kolo Moser, assisted him in the completion of the building complex.

43 Wiedner Hauptstraße

Der Blick vom kleinen Dreieckplatz vor der Paulanerkirche fällt auf den Beginn der Wiedner Hauptstraße. Ausgehend vom Karlsplatz gilt sie seit dem Mittelalter als wichtigste Ausfallstraße nach Süden. Der auf dem alten Foto noch zu sehende, 1846 vor der Paulanerkirche aufgestellte Schutzengelbrunnen von Siccardsburg/Van der Nüll wurde 1963 stadteinwärts auf den Rilkeplatz übertragen und durch eine barocke Maria-Immaculata-Figur ersetzt.

The view from the small triangular space in front of the Paulanerkirche (Church of the Holy Angels) is toward the beginning of the Wiedner Hauptstraße. Commencing from the Karlsplatz, it has been considered to be the most important arterial road to the south since the Middle Ages. The Guardian Angel Fountain, built in front of the Paulanerkirche in 1846 by Siccardsburg/Van der Nüll and visible on the old photo, was moved to the Rilkeplatz in 1963 and replaced by a Baroque figure of Mary Immaculate.

44 Mozartbrunnen
Mozart Fountain

Der von Carl Wollek und Otto Schönthal (Schüler Otto Wagners) gestaltete Mozartbrunnen wurde 1905 enthüllt und erinnert an die Uraufführung der „Zauberflöte" 1791 im Freihaustheater. Die beiden Bronzefiguren zeigen Tamino und Pamina aus Mozarts wohl bekanntester Oper. Einstmals war der Brunnen von einem geschlossenen Biedermeier-Ensemble umgeben, das allerdings in den 1970er Jahren durch die Errichtung eines Wohnbaus ein völlig neues Gesicht erhalten hat.

The Mozart Fountain, designed by Carl Wollek and Otto Schönthal (a student of Otto Wagner), was unveiled in 1905 and commemorates the premiere of "The Magic Flute" in 1791 at the Freihaustheater. The two bronze figures depict Tamino and Pamina from Mozart's arguably most popular opera. Formerly the fountain was surrounded by a complete Biedermeier ensemble. The construction of a residential building in the 1970s, however, gave it an entirely new face.

45 Margarethenplatz

Der Umriss des für den 5. Bezirk namengebenden Margarethenplatzes hat sich seit dem frühen 18. Jh. nicht mehr verändert. Ebenso den Platz dominierend wie das frühere, heute nur noch in Bruchstücken vorhandene Schloss ist seit 1884/85 der Margarethenhof von Fellner und Helmer, von dem aus das Foto gemacht wurde. Es zeigt den Platz mit dem zentralen Margarethenbrunnen (Johann Schaller, 1836), der 1886 im Zuge der Platzregulierung seinen heutigen, inzwischen nicht mehr von einer Straßenbahn umfahrenen Standort erhielt.

The perimeter of the Margarethenplatz, from which the name of the 5th District is derived, has not changed since the early 18th century. Since 1884/85, the Margaretenhof, built by Fellner and Helmer, has dominated the square just as the castle – of which now only ruins remain – used to. The photograph was taken from the Margaretenhof and shows the square with its central fountain Margarethenbrunnen (Johann Schaller, 1836) that was moved to its current location in 1886 in the course of renovations to the square and is no longer circled by a streetcar.

46 Flohmarkt
Flea Market

Am Gelände zwischen Rechter und Linker Wienzeile direkt im Anschluss an den Naschmarkt, Wiens größtem Obst- und Gemüsemarkt, findet seit 1977 jeden Samstag vor dem Hintergrund prächtiger Jugendstilbauten der Flohmarkt statt. Der Handel mit gebrauchten Kleidungsstücken und Alltagsgegenständen ist in Wien bereits seit dem Mittelalter dokumentiert. Heute bieten mehr als 400 Aussteller, darunter auch zahlreiche Antiquitäten- und Altwarenhändler, ihre Ware feil.

Since 1977, the flea market has been held every Saturday against the background of splendid Art Nouveau buildings on the grounds between the Right and Left Wienzeile, directly adjoining the Naschmarkt, Vienna´s largest fruit and vegetable market. Trade in used clothing and in everyday objects has been documented in Vienna already since the Middle Ages. Today more than 400 vendors, among them numerous antiques- and second-hand dealers, offer their goods for sale.

47 Mariahilferstraße

Die seit dem späten 19. Jh. als wichtigste Geschäftsstraße der Vorstädte geltende Mariahilferstraße geht auf einen bereits in der Römerzeit angelegten Straßenzug nach Westen zurück. Innerhalb des Gürtels fungiert sie als Trennung der beiden Bezirke Mariahilf und Neubau, und nach dem Westbahnhof führt sie bis zur Schönbrunner Schlossallee. Der größte Teil der Verbauung besteht aus spätgründerzeitlichen Wohn- und Geschäftshäusern, wie dem seit 1872 existierenden Hotel Kummer, das 1904 durch Ludwig Schwarz neu errichtet wurde.

The Mariahilferstraße, considered to be the principal shopping street in the periphery since the late 19th century, dates back to a Roman road to the west. Within the Gürtel, the street functions as a dividing line between the Mariahilf and Neubau Districts, and it leads to the Schönbrunner Schlossallee from the Westbahnhof. The greater portion of the development consists of late "foundation era" residential and commercial buildings, such as the Hotel Kummer, existing since 1872, built anew in 1904 by Ludwig Schwarz.

48 Volkstheater
People's Theater

Das Volkstheater wurde 1889 als bürgerliches Gegenstück zum Hofburgtheater gegründet und von den meistbeschäftigten Theaterarchitekten der damaligen Zeit, Ferdinand Fellner und Hermann Helmer, im Stil der Neorenaissance erbaut. Die 1945 zerbombte Kuppel und der nach dem Krieg entfernte Fassadendekor wurden bei der Generalsanierung 1980/81 wieder hergestellt. Das ursprünglich vor dem Haupteingang stehende Ferdinand-Raimund-Denkmal ist an den Rand des nahe gelegenen Weghuberparks versetzt worden.

The Volkstheater was founded in 1889 as a civic counterpart to the Imperial Palace Theater and built in the Neo-Renaissance style by the busiest theater architects of the day, Ferdinand Fellner and Hermann Helmer. The dome, destroyed in 1945, and the façade decorations, removed after the war, were restored in the course of the general restoration in 1980/81. The Ferdinand Raimund Memorial which originally stood in front of the main entrance was moved to the edge of the nearby Weghuberpark.

49 Jörgerbad

Der Originalzustand des 1912–14 von Heinrich Goldemund, Friedrich Jäckel und den für Technik und Bauleitung zuständigen Franz Wejmola errichteten Jörgerbades in Hernals ist trotz einer umfassenden Restaurierung in den 70er Jahren kaum angetastet worden. Einzig die Umbenennung von „Städtisches Bad" in „Städtisches Jörgerbad" fällt an der Fassade auf. Auch die Ausstattung der schönen glasüberdachten Schwimmhalle blieb weitgehend erhalten.

In spite of an extensive renovation in the 1970s, the original state of the Jörgerbad (Jörger Pool), constructed between 1912 and 1914 in Hernals by Heinrich Goldemund, Friedrich Jäckel, and site engineer Franz Wejmola, remains largely intact. The only noticeable change on the façade is the pool's renaming from "Municipal Pool" to "Jörger Municipal Pool." Even the décor of the lovely glass-roofed indoor pool was for the most part preserved.

50 Hernals

Dieses traditionelle, inzwischen von einem anderen Besitzer bewirtschaftete Weinhaus an der Ecke Hernalser Hauptstraße/Nesselgasse erinnert an die Zeit, als der entlang des Alserbaches bzw. der Als gelegene Bezirk Hernals ein bedeutendes Weinbaugebiet war. Nach der 1899 abgeschlossenen Kanalisation der Als ist davon – bis auf einen letzten Rest am Schafberg – nichts mehr übrig geblieben. Es gibt jedoch aus damaliger Zeit eine regionale Weinspezialität, den „Alsegger", einen Riesling, der heute noch beim Dornbacher Pfarrer ausgeschenkt wird.

This traditional wine house on the corner of Hernalser Haupstraße and Nesselgasse, which is now managed by a new owner, is reminiscent of the times when the district of Hernals – which lies along the Alserbach and the Als river – was an important wine-growing area. After the canalization of the Als river was completed in 1899, almost nothing of it remained except a tiny rest on the Schafberg. However, there is one regional specialty wine remaining from those times: the "Alsegger," a Riesling, that is still served by the parish priest in Dornbach.

51 Währingerstraße

Vom heute platzartig erweiterten Bereich vor der Pfarrkirche St. Gertrud ist der in der Währinger-straße lückenlos erhaltene Bestand an gründerzeitlichen Zinshäusern besonders gut zu erkennen. Entlang dieser bis 1894 Hauptstraße genannten alten Ausfallstraße entwickelten sich die mittelalterlichen Dörfer Währing und Weinhaus. Der mächtige Turm im Hintergrund gehört zur Pfarrkirche Weinhaus, einem nach Plänen des Dombaumeisters Friedrich von Schmidt 1883–89 errichteten neogotischen Bau.

The almost completely intact and well-preserved stock of Gründerzeit (Foundation Era) apartment houses in the Währingerstraße can be seen spotted especially well from the area in front of the St. Gertrud parish church. The medieval villages Währing and Weinhaus developed along the old arterial road that was called Hauptstraße until 1894. The large tower in the background belongs to the Weinhaus parish church, a Neo-Gothic building that was constructed in 1883–89 according to plans by the master cathedral builder Friedrich von Schmidt.

52 Volksoper
People's Opera

Die 1898 von Franz von Krauß und Alexander Graf errichtete Volksoper war ursprünglich als Sprechbühne geführt und nannte sich „Kaiser-Jubiläums-Stadttheater". Dementsprechend war sie auch nach dem allgemeinen Theaterschema von Fellner und Helmer, den Erbauern des Volkstheaters, geplant worden. Opern und Singspiele sind erst ab 1903 auf dem Spielplan zu finden. Der Platz vor der zur Währingerstraße schräg gestellten Hauptfassade wurde durch die Zinshausverbauung am Gürtel (Baubeginn 1893) erheblich verkleinert.

The Volksoper, built in 1898 by Franz von Krauß and Alexander Graf, was originally a stage for drama and was called the "Kaiser-Jubiläums-Stadttheater" (Emperor's Jubilee City Theater). Correspondingly, it was planned according to the general theater plans of Fellner and Helmer, the builders of the Volkstheater. Standard and singspiel operas joined the repertoire only in 1903. The square in front of the main façade, diagonal to the Währingerstraße, was considerably reduced through the construction of revenue properties on the Gürtel beginning in 1893.

53 Strudelhofstiege
Strudelhof Steps

Die pittoreske, mit Vasen, Wandbrunnen und Kandelabern versehene Treppenanlage wurde durch den Roman „Die Strudelhofstiege" von Heimito von Doderer, an den eine Gedenktafel erinnert, allgemein bekannt. 1910 von Theodor Jäger erbaut, verbindet sie über die Strudelhofgasse die Währinger- mit der Liechtensteinstraße. Unweit von ihr befindet sich das Palais Liechtenstein mit seiner erstklassigen Sammlung barocker Meister.

The picturesque stairway, decorated with vases, fountains and candelabras, became well known through the novel "Die Strudelhofstiege" by Heimito von Doderer who is commemorated there by a plaque. Built in 1910 by Theodor Jäger, it connects the Währingerstraße with the Liechtensteinstraße via the Strudelhofgasse. Nearby is the Liechtenstein Palace with its superb collection of Baroque masterpieces.

54 Roßauer Lände

Das Polizeigefangenenhaus an der Roßauer Lände wurde 1901–04 nach Plänen Emil Ritter von Försters errichtet. Die weitläufige Anlage mit dem markanten, mit secessionistischen Stilelementen ausgestatteten Eckturm liegt am stadtseitigen Donaukanalufer. Nach dem früheren Namen der Roßauer Lände, der Kaiserin-Elisabeth-Promenade, wurde das Polizeigebäude im Volksmund nahezu liebevoll „Liesl" genannt.

The police prison on the Roßauer Lände was built in 1901–04 according to plans by Emil Ritter von Förster. The expansive complex with its distinctive corner tower embellished with Secessionist stylistic elements is located on the city-side of the Donaukanal. The police building was almost affectionately nicknamed "Liesl" by the Viennese after Kaiserin-Elisabeth-Promenade, the previous name of the Roßauer Lände.

55 Praterstern

Das Denkmal für den Begründer der Seemacht der Donaumonarchie, Admiral Tegetthoff, sollte zunächst vor der Votivkirche aufgestellt werden, bevor es schließlich 1886 am Praterstern enthüllt wurde. Carl Kundmann und Carl von Hasenauer hatten mit der 16 m hohen Marmorsäule auf hohem Sockel, bekrönt vom Admiral, die Triumphsäule des antiken Seehelden, die columna rostrata (Schiffsschnäbel) zum Vorbild. Der Volksmund mutmaßte ironisch, es handle sich dabei um das Denkmal für den Erfinder des Kleiderständers.

The monument to the founder of the naval power of the Danube Monarchy, Admiral Tegetthoff, was originally to be erected in front of the Votivkirche. It was ultimately unveiled at the Praterstern in 1886. Carl Kundmann and Carl von Hasenauer modeled the 16m (53 ft) high marble column on a high pedestal, crowned by the admiral, on triumphal columns of naval heroes of classical antiquity, the columna rostrata (prows). An ironic vernacular interpretation speculated that on top of this column was a monument to the inventor of the clothes tree.

56 Riesenrad
Ferris Wheel

Das 1896 von Walter B. Basset of Watermouth und Hitchins erbaute Riesenrad ist das neben dem Stephansdom bekannteste Wahrzeichen Wiens. Es dominiert den so genannten Wurstelprater, einen Teil des ehemaligen kaiserlichen Jagdgebiets östlich des Pratersterns, der 1766 durch Kaiser Joseph II. öffentlich zugänglich gemacht wurde. Nach einem Brand 1945 wurde dieser Vergnügungspark vollständig zerstört und in veränderter Form wieder aufgebaut. Dabei ist auch die Anzahl der Riesenrad-Waggons um die Hälfte reduziert worden.

In addition to St. Stephen's Cathedral, the Giant Ferris Wheel, built by Walter B. Basset of Watermouth and Hitchins in 1896, is Vienna's most famous landmark. It dominates the so-called "Wurstelprater", a part of the former imperial hunting grounds to the east of the Praterstern, made publicly accessible after 1766 by Emperor Joseph II. After a fire in 1945 this amusement park was entirely destroyed and rebuilt in a new form. In the course of this, the number of coaches on the ferris wheel was reduced by half.

57 Volksprater

Das Restaurant „Zum Walfisch" im Volksprater erhielt seinen Namen wegen eines 1895 erleg-
ten Pottwals, mit dessen Teilen, die sich heute im Pratermuseum befinden, das Restaurant
ausgeschmückt war. Die prächtige Arkadenfront auf dem alten Foto gehörte zur gleichnamigen, 1898 eröffneten Grottenbahn. Sie war die erste elektrisch betriebene Grottenbahn Europas und soll eine Fläche von 3000 m² gehabt haben. Sie wurde beim Großbrand des traditi-
onsreichen, seit 1766 existierenden Vergnügungsviertels 1945 zerstört.

The restaurant "Zum Walfisch" ("The Whale") in the Volksprater was named after a sperm
whale caught in 1895, whose parts, today on display in the Pratermuseum, decorated the
restaurant. The grand arcaded front on the old photo belonged to the Grottenbahn (Grotto
Train), opened in 1898. It was the first electric grotto train in Europe and is said to have had a
surface area of 3000 m² (32,290 ft²). In 1945 it was destroyed in a devastating fire in the old
amusement district, which dated back to 1766.

58 Lusthaus
Pleasure House

Das Lusthaus am Ende der Prater Hauptallee in der Freudenau wurde 1781–83 im Auftrag
Josefs II. von Isidoro Canevale errichtet und nach einem Bombentreffer 1945 in reduzierter
Form 1948/49 wieder aufgebaut. Oftmals Schauplatz opulenter Festlichkeiten, ist heute im acht-
eckigen, von kolossalen Rundpfeilern umgebenen Zentralbau ein Restaurant untergebracht.

The Pleasure House at the end of the Prater's main avenue in Freudenau was commissioned
by Josef II and built between 1781–1783 by Isidoro Canevale. After being struck by a bomb in
1945, it was reconstructed in a reduced form between 1948/49. The frequent site of opulent
festivities in the past, the central building now houses an octagonal restaurant, which is surrounded by large rounded pillars.

59   Schönbrunn

Das 1997 in die Liste des Kulturerbes der UNESCO aufgenommene Schloss Schönbrunn mit seinen großzügigen Gärten und dem ältesten Tiergarten der Welt gehört zu den bedeutendsten barocken Anlagen Europas. Das Bild zeigt den 1996 in den Ostflügel verlegten Haupteingang mit seinen charakteristischen, von Adlern bekrönten Obelisken und den um 1700 von Johann Bernhard Fischer von Erlach ausgeführten Mitteltrakt. Im Wesentlichen vollendet wurde das Schloss nach 1750 unter Maria Theresia durch Nikolaus Pacassi und im frühen 19.Jh. durch den Klassizisten Johann Aman.

Added to UNESCO's list of world heritage sites in 1997, Schloss Schönbrunn – with its expansive gardens and the oldest zoo in the world – is considered one of the most significant Baroque ensembles in Europe. The photograph shows the main entrance – relocated to the East Wing in 1996 – with its characteristic eagle-crowned obelisks, and the central wing that was constructed around 1700 by Johann Bernhard Fischer von Erlach. The palace was essentially completed after 1750 under the rule of Maria Theresia by Nikolaus Pacassi and then by the classicist Johann Aman in the early 19th century.

60   Kahlenberg

Der Kahlenberg (484 m) und der steil zur Donau abfallende Leopoldsberg (424 m) sind die Wiener Hausberge. Sie liegen im nördlichen Wienerwald und bilden die Stadtgrenze zu Klosterneuburg. Ursprünglich hieß der Leopoldsberg Kahlenberg und der Kahlenberg wegen des reichen Wildschweinbestandes Sauberg, bis Kaiser Leopold I. im 17. Jh. die Umbenennung vornahm. Der seit 1935 durch die Höhenstraße erreichbare Kahlenberg ist wegen seines schönen Ausblickes auf Wien stark frequentiertes Ausflugsziel.

The Kahlenberg (484 m /1,585 ft) and the Leopoldsberg (424 m /1,390 ft), which slopes steeply toward the Danube are Vienna's "own" mountains. They are located in the northern Vienna Woods and form the city boundary to Klosterneuburg. Originally the Leopoldsberg was named Kahlenberg, and the Kahlenberg was called "Sauberg" (Sow Mountain) because of the many wild boars. Emperor Leopold I renamed them in the 17th century. The Kahlenberg, accessible since 1935 via the Höhenstraße (Panorama Road), is a heavily frequented outing destination due to the lovely views of Vienna.

Alexander Pointner, Wien 2006

IMPRESSUM

Edition Fotohof – Herausgegeben von Kurt Kaindl
Band 31: Wien gestern und heute
Herausgegeben von Maria Emberger
Fotografie: László Lugo Lugosi
Kommentar: Alexander Pointner

Für diesen Bildband wurden Fotografien aus den Beständen der Sammlung Seemann, Wien, der Postkartensammlung des „Zempléni Muzem", Szerencs, Ungarn und aus der Sammlung László Lugo Lugosi, Budapest, Ungarn verwendet, die Inhaber sämtlicher Bildrechte sind. Die Aufnahmen aus den Jahren 2005/06 stammen von László Lugo Lugosi, die Bildrechte liegen beim Autor. Kontakt: www.lugophoto.com

Wir bedanken uns bei Budapest Galéria, Collegium Hungaricum, Alte Schmiede Kunstverein, Pál Deréky, Helfried Seemann und János Lukács.

Umschlaggestaltung unter Verwendung eines Fotos von László Lugo Lugosi und eines Fotos aus dem Bestand seiner Sammlung.
Lektorat: Karoline Neubauer (Otto Müller Verlag, Salzburg)
Übersetzungen: Susanna Seidl-Fox, Salzburg, Kathleen Sagmeister-Fox, Lochau
Layout: Moni Kaszta
Gestaltung: Hermann Resch, Salzburg
Lithos: László Lugo Lugosi, Budapest, Color Photo Digital, Budapest, Repro 4C, Salzburg
Druck: Druckerei Theiss GmbH, St. Stefan im Lavanttal

ISBN-10: 3-7013-1124-2 · ISBN-13: 978-3-7013-1124-8
© 2006 Otto Müller Verlag, Salzburg/Wien und bei den Autoren

IMPRINT

Edition Fotohof – Edited by Kurt Kaindl
Volume 31: Vienna then and now
Edited by Maria Emberger
Photography: László Lugo Lugosi
Comments: Alexander Pointner

Photographs from the holdings of the Seeman Collection, Vienna, the postcard collection of the "Zempléni Muzem" Szerencs, Hungary, and the László Lugo Lugosi Collection, Budapest, Hungary, which also own their copyright, were used for this volume. Photographs from the years 2005/2006 were taken by László Lugo Lugosi, who owns their copyright. Contact: www.lugophoto.com

We would like to thank the Budapest Galéria, the Collegium Hungaricum, the Alte Schmiede Kunstverein, Pál Deréky, Helfried Seemann and János Lukács.

Cover design using a photograph by László Lugo Lugosi and a photograph from the holdings of the László Lugo Lugosi Collection, Vienna.
Copy-editor: Karoline Neubauer (Otto Müller Verlag, Salzburg)
Translations: Kathleen Sagmeister-Fox, Lochau, and Susanna Seidl-Fox, Salzburg
Layout: Moni Kaszta
Design: Hermann Resch, Salzburg
Lithos: László Lugo Lugosi, Budapest, Color Photo Digital, Budapest, Repro 4C, Salzburg
Printing: Druckerei Theiss GmbH, St. Stefan im Lavanttal

ISBN-10: 3-7013-1124-2 · ISBN-13: 978-3-7013-1124-8
© 2006 Otto Müller Verlag, Salzburg/Vienna and the authors